ANCIENT ROME

THE RISE AND FALL OF THE ROMAN KINGDOM

Victor Miller

TABLE OF CONTENTS

legal responsibility or blame be held against the publisher for any reparation, damages, or monetary loss due to the information herein, either directly or indirectly.

Respective authors own all copyrights not held by the publisher.

The information herein is offered for informational purposes solely, and is universal as so. The presentation of the information is without contract or any type of guarantee assurance.

The trademarks that are used are without any consent, and the publication of the trademark is without permission or backing by the trademark owner. All trademarks and brands within this book are for clarifying purposes only and are the owned by the owners themselves, not affiliated with this document.

INTRODUCTION

I want to thank you and congratulate you on downloading *"Ancient Rome: The Rise and Fall of the Roman Kingdom"*.

In this book we will take a walk down the decorated lane of Roman history. It will give you an in depth look at the grandiose life of the Romans and give you a profound perspective on the contributions they made to the world we live in today.

It's safe to say that while the Ancient Romans are separated from our lives today by thousands of years, it is impossible to imagine a modern Europe without Roman flavor and influence. Believe it or not, much of the quality of life we experience today comes from what the Romans gave to us all those years ago.

To those who take a keen interest in the histories of great nations, they might be surprised to learn that the model Romans followed, for better or for worse, was adhered to many generations thereafter. What was it about the Romans that made them so influential, so compelling? While you travel through this narrative retracing the glorious lives of Romans, consider what makes them so attractive to our imaginations. Why were they so powerful? Why are we still engaged millennia later? And finally, what is it that we share with them today and what makes us different from them?

One reason that made the Roman Empire so magnificent is that it was a symbol of ultimate success to any nation that harbored imperialist ambitions, especially Britain. Many nations all over Europe, including those in the Mediterranean, went on to replicate the Roman model, but could never quite match it. They inspired great leaders not only in their attempts at conquest but also in their inroads to peace and unity across conquered lands.

But power corrupts, and absolute power corrupts absolutely, and over the years, from one leader to another, the Roman model began to alter and become increasingly tyrannical. Dream of a flourishing Roman empire became just that— a dream. Dictators such as Mussolini became infatuated by the lure of power inherent in the great Roman Empire, but did not consider the most essential part of the equation – Rome's understanding of peace, prosperity and harmony. By the 20th century, the Roman style of conquest would become distorted with newfangled ideas. The rule became centralized, local identities became suppressed, and the imposition of a "unified" belief system became a common practice. The human population was reduced to the status of slaves, subjugated people were exploited, and women were deprived of all their political rights. Soon the dreamlike model became a nightmare for the people who fell under the rule of these whimsical leaders.

The Europe we know today is said to be resting on the laurels of Ancient Roman Empire. The 2000-year-old history that separates us from their decorated past has been glorified in so many ways that we've christened it the 'Eternal City'. After all, if the Romans are to be believed, they date all the way back to 753 BC.

As we delve deeper into the ancient times of Rome and the empire that was built during those years, all we ask is this one question: Why is it worthy of our attention? The only way one can justifiably answer this rhetorical question is with an oratorical answer: It was one of the greatest powers of the ancient world with insurmountable influence that dictated not one but arguably all modern nations.

In conjunction with the Ancient Greeks and Hebrews, Romans offer a lot to this world in terms of illustrious history. Imagine a world where these people did not even exist. To say that our lives, myths, customs, cultures, and existence would be different is an epic understatement.

If you want to take a nose dive into the modern day world and understand where we are, then you need to know where our current culture stems from. This is where Roman history comes into play. Our literature, language, religion, art, government, and law, all comes from the rules that were established centuries ago by the Roman people.

From humble beginnings, Rome would go on to become a world leader and one of the world's great cities; and while the successful empire built around it faced multiple challenges, Rome would leave an inextricable mark in history.

In this book, we will look at all the unique features that defined Ancient Rome. Social division was one of the important things in the Roman world – the structure of the classes was critical for this cosmopolitan city, where each individual needed to know and respect their own place. From the slaves to the plebeians and the mighty equestrians, everyone was ruled by patricians.

Another important feature of Rome was, and still is, its government. Filled with bureaucracy in the later years and simple yet complex after the merger of the three tribes, the city of seven hills knew how to keep everyone in their place, recording every grain and slave which passed through the city gates. Their successful democracy lasted longer than any other, to this date.

It boggles the mind to imagine the arc of Ancient Rome. The first Rome had just a couple of rather humble huts and one protection wall. Early Rome was nothing compared to the epic city it was to become— the city to which all roads lead. This infrastructure, too, was one of the multiple particularities of Rome, making it one-of-a-kind in a world of "barbarians" who lived on land with roads that linked two villages at the most. There was no capital, only multiple, isolated tribes. With Rome, things changed: all the roads lead to one powerful and highly demanding city that required an enormous amount of resources to function.

Thanks again for downloading this book, I hope you enjoy it!

I

THE LEGEND OF ROMULUS AND REMUS

A river runs through an isolated place, nourishing mankind and the animal world alike. The year is around 700 before the birth of Christ; the wind is blowing, the river is swelling with the annual flood, and a dark, stooping man—probably a servant— is carrying a basket large enough to hold the two twin newborn boys it houses. The servant is walking down the river bank, taking each step carefully – he must not wake the babies, so recently separated from their mother and cursed by her uncle. Cursed because they were born despite the vow of celibacy their mother was forced into to protect the uncle's kingdom. She had kept mum despite the cruelty he had shown to her father (the actual ruler) and also kept silent when the throne was forcibly taken away from her father. But this time, she could not keep quiet. She had begged the servant not to kill them, as her uncle had mercilessly ordered him to; after all, there was a prophecy which stated that the twins would have him overthrown. The servant pitied the poor souls, agreeing to take them away from their wailing mother, imprisoned and enchained for her accidental motherhood.

Taking them to the river Tiber, he wonders what will become of the babies, for the river banks are full of wild animals, cannibal tribes, and a dozen other dangers even grown men of great valor cannot survive. It is likely these newborn babies will be finished in seconds. As he kneels beside the river to set them off on a river safari of their own, he says a little prayer – "Help them, it is not their fault." Turning away from the floating basket, he wipes away a tear, and sets off back to the king's abode.

The river flows and flows and soon, begins to flood and overflow, luckily for the babies. The basket lands on the banks several miles away from where they were set off and, miraculously, stays put.

Divine coincidence provides – a she-wolf has lost her cubs and is grieving when she hears the babies crying through the woods. She is not human, but understands a baby's wails when she hears them. Curiosity makes her take a look, and she finds the babies, wailing and starving! Her motherly instinct kicks in, dictating that she accept the children – she feeds them her milk, cleans them... in some sense, nature has returned her cubs.

These are the royal children Romulus and Remus – born to Rhea Silvia, the daughter of Numitor, king of Alba Longa. His brother Amulius, Rhea's uncle has taken the kingdom away from Numitor and killed his only son to make sure the kingdom remains his. This is why Rhea was forced to become a vestal virgin, so that there would be no more heirs. When Amulius learned that Rhea was pregnant with Mars' babies, as she declared, he was furious, as it spelled doom to his unobstructed ownership of the throne. He imprisoned her and tortured her. But the babies were born, and, when he tried to get them killed, they were washed ashore and nourished by the she wolf, later to be brought up by Fastulus and his wife.

Romulus and Remus grew up to be fine men and went on to avenge their family against Amelius for the atrocities he had committed on their grandfather and mother. They managed to overthrow him, give the kingdom back to Numitor, and go on to establish the city of Rome – the root of all greatness. The river god of Tiber, Tiberinus was kind to Rhea and married her.

This is the story of how one of the most popular, influential, and significant civilizations – Rome as we know it—began. Although this is a mere legend used to describe the dawn of this civilization, it is an engaging and enticing opening scene to what will come. Prehistory is all unrecorded history, travelling into the present in the form of fables and stories historians disregard due to lack of proof. But while illusory, they create an amazing backdrop in the cultural sense and introduce the society to come in an evocative and compelling way.

Romans stemmed from Alba Longa, with further connections to the ancient city of Troy in Asia Minor. The great fire burnt the city and a Trojan hero Aeneas escaped with his father on his shoulders and son in his arms. Landing on the Italian mainland, he went on to establish the city of Latvinium, which provides the connection to the Alba Longa we have been talking about. Aeneas's descendants are Numitor and Amulius – and the sons of Rhea Silvia are the next generation. They were washed on the shores of what we now know as Rome; after Romulus had killed his brother in an argument, he became the king of the new city.

This is the story of the founding of Rome, and it is the stuff of legend, literally. The foundation myth of Rome was drafted by Greek historians initially. In keeping with their usual approach to the histories of their neighbors, the Greeks used their own myths and archetypes to dress out this story about Romulus and Remus. From the 5th century B.C., Greek historians and writers used a wide variety of myths to account for the start of Rome. One popular version stems from the legend of the Trojan hero Aeneas. After he and his followers left Troy and began wandering the Mediterranean, they finally settled in Italy. Soon, they were marrying locals and creating families, and would eventually become the tribe known as the Latins.

This connection between Ancient Troy and Rome is a story, but it was a resonant story for later Romans. The Roman historians who came to prominence during the Republic used Greek methods for tracking genealogy and the barebones records they had left from the time to create a timeline for the early kings and the start of Rome. These methods established the "official" start date of Rome as around 753 B.C.; however, this was still nearly half a millennium from the days of Aeneas. In order to compensate for this gap in the record, Roman historians developed a complex maze of myth, tracing a path from the early Latins to Rome over 400 years later through a series of legendary and mostly fictional kings. This line eventually led to Romulus and Remus, the last in a long royal line that traced its roots back to Troy.

This legend marks the beginning of the Roman Empire, dated by most accounts to around 750 BC. Romans to this day consider Romulus to be their ancestor. From this legendary start, let us now embark on the exciting journey of discovering and discussing the unfolding of a great empire.

THE ITALY OF EARLY ROME

What was the actual Italy like in the time in which Romulus was alleged to have lived? It was a multicultural collection of different tribes, cultures, religions, and languages. The vast majority of Italy was agrarian, and the smattering of small villages and towns were dominated by subsistence farmers. These farmers sowed the earth, kept and bred animals, and lived a minimal life with little interaction with anyone beyond the nearest village.

The various tribes spread across Italy spoke several dialects stemming from the Indo-European family of languages. These included Oscan, Umbrian, Latin, and Venetic. The Etruscans stood apart, speaking a non-Indo European language as did the Gallic tribes of the North. The south of Italy saw a smattering of Greek settlements, who engaged in trade with the various tribes across Italy.

This world was a limited world, a world of subsistence and day to day needs. While the Greeks engaged in trade, the majority of Italian tribes maintained a more limited sphere. The Etruscans were the ambitious ones in the Italian group, developing the first, world-class culture in the region.

It was only through the influence of the Greeks and Etruscans that the Rome we would come to know came about. The tribes of central Italy borrowed the best of the Etruscans and Greeks, adopting everything from their alphabet to the regalia these cultures used in ceremony. Things we think of today as iconic of Rome were actually Etruscan in origin, including the toga praetexta and gladiator combat. It was in this melting pot of cultures that the earliest days of Rome occurred, and it was this very diversity that gave it its unique flavor and strength.

II

THE CORE AREAS OF THE ROMAN LIFE

Roman society was held together with religion, an aspect of culture that was all-pervasive and all-important in Roman times. Religion manifested itself throughout the various levels of the society, beginning first with the family.

The family was headed by the father, making Rome at heart a patriarchal society. As the head of the Roman family, the father was in charge of all religious rites and also controlled the children. A strong bond among the family members prevailed, and everyone looked up to the man of the house for advice and direction. Interestingly, the concept of adopted children was acceptable in Roman society as well, and these children also thrived under the administrative care of the father, the 'pater familias'. The mother had little or no right in making family decisions. The adult sons also fell under the control of the pater familias, as an adult son could not become an authority figure himself until his father died, while adult daughters fell under the pater familias of her husband's home. In a striking difference to most modern societies, the Roman pater familias also had the right to even kill a family member as punishment. He was the supreme authority, and could force divorce or marriage, and even sell children into slavery. Affection towards children was never shown.

Marriage was a matter of political and economic advantage, and had none of the romance or sentiment we associate with it today. The moment girls hit puberty, they were looked on as would–be brides, likely to be married to an older man. This rule did not apply to the lower caste women, who often married later in their twenties. Women had no choices—the husband could be chosen by the pater familias only.

Unwanted children were often sold into slavery. Children were brought up by the mother or any other elderly relative of the family, but the pater familias did not bother with this issue. Overall, the approach to parenting and taking care of a family in Rome was one of pragmatism.

Roman society also allowed for larger groups of families, known as The Gens. The Gens were defined through common descent or adoption ties. They performed the same religious rites and could also serve as political alliances. In fact, using Gens for political purposes would become quite popular as the Roman timeline moved forward. Encompassing multiple Gens that all worshipped the same God was The Curia. Finally, the collection of various Curia made the Tribe.

THE ROMAN WORLD

History is rife with the stories casting Romans as the true conquerors of the world. The Roman narrative, however, is not just one of domination, but also one of unification. Rome not only conquered some of the most popular countries of the old world but also made them all into a single unified entity – the Roman World. All the countries that bordered the Mediterranean Sea – Palestine and Syria, Macedonia and Greece, Egypt and Carthage, became part of a single Roman Empire. All these countries followed the same ideas and customs, and had similar art and religion. As a result, all these nations welded together to form the integrated whole that we know as the Roman civilization. Looking at their successful history in this respect, it is safe to say that Romans were indeed one of the most triumphant cultures in the ancient world.

BUILDING A SOCIETY OF SLAVES

There are many things about Rome and its gifts to the world today that we like to celebrate long after their fall. However, there are also parts of the history that put its magnificent past to shame. The slave society that was built by the overzealous rulers is one of the elements that separate us from the world that the Roman Empire constructed back in the day.

Slavery was an important part of the Roman history, defining many aspects of Roman society as well as its economy. However, unlike the slavery belonging to the American Plantation, they did not go so far as to divide the populace based on race or color; partition came as a direct result of an invasion. But as in American slavery, the slave was considered property, a thing which the owner could use, give as a gift, sell and even discard, which in the case of the slave might mean death.

In this respect, when we look back at the Roman world we see it not as a model that we would like to replicate today but an alternative that terrifies and is best kept locked in the history books. During this reign of terror, humans lost their basic rights and were subjected to physical punishment as well as judicial torture. In extreme cases, they were even put to death.

The rebel slaves were led to death by crucifixion and were killed in the thousands, while some met their end in a ghastly manner and put in the arena for entertainment of people. Brutality became a necessary evil and an accepted part of the system, not something that people objected to or scorned. The slave trade became all the more consequential to the Roman civilization because most of its economy depended on it.

This system that seems cruel and intolerable was tolerated by the Roman people for centuries. It did provoke a few cases of rebellion by the slaves but no extraordinary protest was recorded or survived in the records we have today. The only reason that made this repressive state seemingly reasonable to the people was that slaves were allowed freedom after some time and could gain legal status as a full citizen with all the subsequent rights once a slave owner gave up ownership of a slave. This system of manumission was encouraged primarily because it gave slaves hope and encouraged them to work harder. Freedmen did not have the right to vote, but their children would, providing even more fuel to the fire and stoking many a slave's ambitions.

The freed slaves had the opportunity to work their way up and get promoted to the master class. The ones who thrived in the world of business and commerce were the examples of the incentive of working with the system rather than revolting against it.

Roman society became known for its paradoxes. The freemen served the emperors alongside the slaves, and as they rose through the ranks they also wielded exceptional power and influence; so much so, that even the most prominent people had to pay them court.

THE LIFE OF THE ROMAN SLAVE

To understand Rome, you need to understand the unique life of the slave in the ancient city. The concept of "slave" in Rome was very different from how we understand it today. Our modern perception is profoundly influenced by the U.S. narrative, a racially-driven system of oppression. Slaves in Rome, however, were not separated from free men by race. In fact, slaves in Rome could come from anywhere, even the children of Romans.

Slaves came from all aspects of Roman life. Most often, they came from the battlefield as prisoners. Slaves could come from inside Rome, too, however, particularly in the form of children. Orphaned or abandoned children were often sold into slavery as were the children of families in need of money.

Any wealthy Roman looking for a slave went to the central marketplace to purchase one. The most valuable slaves were young men with a skill or trade, with cooks going for a particularly pretty penny. Any purchased slave could also buy his or her freedom, though being able to save this sum was all but impossible. Slaves who married and started a family condemned their children as well to a life of slavery. In some cases, pregnant slaves took desperate measures to avoid cursing their children to this fate.

The number of slaves in Rome can only be guessed at. A "middle-class" household might have one or two, while a wealthy Roman could own hundreds. It is thought that a King or Emperor at any given time might have had slaves in the thousands, if not tens of thousands. Slaves were often well cared for, as they were valuable commodities, but by and large as much as 25 percent of the Roman population was living in the desperate straits of complete servitude.

The daily life of a Roman slave probably ran along these lines: Her morning began early, with the slave responsible for priming the environment so that it was as comfortable as possible by the time master awoke. Starting fires, for example, were a top priority. A slave might dress a master or mistress when they awoke or else pursue one of the endless list of daily tasks needed to keep a household running. Cooking food, doing the gardening, or even washing clothes may have been in order.

Large social events were an essential part of Roman life as well, and holding an event required the work of many slaves. Slaves would help bathe all members of a household, bear the litter if the mistress needed to run an errand, and prepare all of the food and settings. Slaves were also obliged to see after the needs of any guests, including walking them home safely after the evening's festivities. The one upside of a long night's work was that banquets often afforded slaves some of the best meals they would have all year, and masters often allowed slaves to enjoy the excess bounty of these epic feasts.

Slaves had important roles outside the Roman home, as well. In fact, the entire Roman economy depended on slave labor. Everything from farms to mines was worked by these enslaved people, and every major government infrastructure project was built by slaves. Slaves were an undeniable and ever-present part of Roman life. Rome worked to keep them integrated into society, never stigmatizing them out of fear that this would provide slaves with the fuel they needed to rebel.

Unity in Diversity

One of the most spellbinding aspects of Rome, since its beginnings as a Kingdom till became an Empire was its control over the diversity that expanded across several geographical as well as cultural landscapes. The Roman Empire is considered a European empire because back in the day, it ruled most of the territories that belong to the present day European Union. The only nations that did not fall under its rule were Germany and the countries of Scandinavia.

Overall, the Roman Empire was also considered a Mediterranean realm that found unity in its diversity. Managing a wide expanse of assorted cultures like Asia, Egypt, and North Africa resulted in a fine mix of customs and traditions living in absolute harmony. The languages that prevailed across the region were Latin and Greek. The various regions soon started gaining status through their growing cities, gaining their first formal apparatus of entertainment and public service and advancing them to 'first world' status.

The ancient Roman Empire worked wonders when it came to effectively maintaining a city-based civilization while also maintaining common cultural values, even in societies that were as diverse as the ones that made up the Empire.

The reason that can be attributed to the seamless functioning of the states despite their diversity was their self-governing nature. Even though there were hints of regional conflicts, the emperors did not feel obliged to offer protection. The unity of the empire was largely based on several factors. Since the central state was not as huge as the ones we find in modern day societies, it was much easier to monitor and administer rules.

The main factor, however, that led to the unity of the regions was the participation of the neighboring areas in that central power. Since the emperors came from not just Rome/Italy but also other parts of the region, the uniform economic prosperity exuding from Rome made its way into the lives of people in the form of outward ripples over a period of time.

CLASSES

Patricians were people who were related to or descendants of the mythical Romulus. Plebeians were all other citizens of Rome.

On the basis of financial situation, people could fall under one of these categories.

There were three classes of people who owned certain categories of property and worked hard to pay taxes. The **Senatorial class** had at least 1,000,000 Sestertii (Roman coins). They had a good deal of money and assets but did not engage in any work. **Equites** (**Knights**) had 4,000,000 Sestertii and were the business class. The last, the **Proletarii**, were the poorest in the classification with not more than 11,000 in assets.

There was also, as mentioned earlier, the class of 'Freedmen' who were initially slaves but later freed by their owners. Their children had all the rights of a citizen and could enjoy the benefits of the state.

As the breadth and reach of Rome continued to expand, these basic structures would become more complex. Rome was on its way to becoming the world's first large-scale bureaucracy with and endless list of offices designed to manage an ever-evolving military, political structure, and society.

Rome's historians trace the development of this wide-ranging bureaucracy to the conflict between the Patricians and the Plebeians. In its earliest years, Rome placed the vast majority of power in the hands of the alleged descendants of Romulus, giving the Patricians extensive, even exclusive, powers in the Senate and in religious offices. Plebeians, on the other hand, were limited to voting in assembly, but could not take on other more visible, social roles. The Plebeians eventually grew frustrated with the limitations afforded them by the system, and it was only through their continued advocacy that Rome would eventually develop it's more complex and less elitist system of governance.

How and when Rome first divided its populace into these two major classes is something of a mystery. While legend says the two classes were established under the founder, Romulus, contemporary historians have a hard time establishing a specific timeline. What is known is that by the time of the Republic, there were only a handful of Patrician families left, with families from both classes making up the Roman version of the "noble" class.

III

THE FORMATION OF ROME AS A CAPITAL CITY

Rome's history influenced the entire course of European history, certainly, but what influenced Rome's history? While the Kings and Emperors of Rome built the city step by step, the natural setting had a lot of influence over this majestic city, as well.

THE SEVEN HILLS OF ROME

One of the most prominent features of Rome was the hills that nurtured the city and protected it from dangers, such as pirates and invaders. Rome was built between seven hill formations located eighteen miles away from the river Tiber, making it easy for commercial boats to access the city yet harder for pirates to reach its gates, as few of them ventured onto narrow rivers.

There was a northern formation, comprised of four hills: Capitoline, Quirinal, Viminal and Esquiline. These were set in a semicircle formation, protecting the future city from barbarians who might have come from the North. The second section of hills was comprised of three formations, Palatine, Aventine and Caelian, which formed a triangle. Together with the Northern hills, they formed a circular area where people could settle down and build a strong city. Because the Palatine was the central hill; the establishment brought to life on it was the one that controlled the other mini-cities.

The natural isolation of these hills initially encouraged the establishment of separate settlements on each. These settlements, in a sense, "watched" one another from afar, but had little interaction at first. The archaeological record indicates that each of these hilled encampments had its own protective wall for a time.

One of the first attempts at interaction came in the form of games. The settlements began to participate in religious games and festivals together, creating deeper cultural bonds. Over time, they naturally sought to convene in the central point that connected them all—the valley in between the array of seven hills. This would take some effort, as the land was marshy. By draining the land and making it livable, these early settlements created the stage for a common area, which would become a forum, bonding the settlements further and bringing them together into what would became Rome.

The geography of these Roman hills made it much coveted land and put it within reach of several envious tribes. This early city of the seven hills was located between three large countries, which also left a mark on the people of Rome. To the North there was the land of the Sabines, to the South there was the Latium and to the northwest, across the Tiber, there was Etruria. All of these regions were competing for the best location and extended their boundaries towards the seven hills, the ideal location from a tactical and resourceful point of view.

THE RISE OF ROME AS ONE CITY

As these three countries continued to extend their boundaries in toward the Seven Hills, the Palatine hills were soon "conquered" by the Latins. A small group of Latin farmers came to the Palatine hills, probably from the largest city of Latium, Alba Longa. They might have been sent there as outposts, to protect the Latin border from other tribes or as commercial agents, to trade with the other tribes in the area or both. The Latin tribe, called Ramnes, erected a village and small straw huts, faced towards the Caelian and the Aventine hills. They soon built a masonry wall, which was meant to protect them and their cattle from attacks by other tribes. This wall became known as the "Wall of Romulus", while the entire fortification was called Roma Quadrata, meaning "the square Rome". To this day, the wall built by the Latins on the Palatine is recognized as the oldest fortification in Rome.

While the Romans were building their fortified village on the Palatine, the Sabines were doing the same thing on the Quirinal hills.

It was only a matter of time before the two tribes clashed; when things came to a head, neither force was strong enough to conquer the other village. As the Romans and the Sabines were close to each other and competed for the same resources they were forced to find a way to co-exist. War was not an option, so they united, becoming a single city, on two hills.

The two tribes celebrated the union by adhering to a two-face god, symbolizing their new, two-hill city. The space between the two former villages was used as a forum, being a market place, as well as a place of meeting for people of the new city. The Capitoline was chosen as a sort of capital for the new city.

But Rome was not yet complete – there was a third tribe, called the Luceres. The exact origin of these people is unknown; there are suppositions they were from Etruria, but other historians say they were another branch of the Latins. Either way, the Luceres were living on the Caelian hills and were incorporated by the Romans. The new union, stronger and larger than ever before, created a common religion, politics, and social life and glued the three former tribes together.

By the time mighty Rome was born, all the three regions had left their unique mark – Rome was never a closed city, but a nonconformist, open metropolis, where different cultures and beliefs blended into one unique conscience. As the city grew, it attracted more and more foreigners, gaining more strength, which enabled it to become the strongest city in Italy and in the Old World.

What is unique about this time in particular can be seen in how this growing city dealt with diversity, both in itself and in its relationship with "outsiders". We've already seen that Rome was a hodgepodge of different tribes from its earliest days. What distinguished this new city from other successful cultures in the Ancient World was in how it assimilated new peoples and cultures. This would become the single most defining characteristic of the eventual Roman Empire, and its early seeds are evident here.

This is also clear in how Rome dealt with the powerful Etruscans to the north. While a culture such as Greece sought to conquer lands and "Hellenize" them, making them Greek, Rome assimilated new cultures into its already complex melting pot. We shall discuss how the mighty Etruscans kept a dominant hand over this early Rome for a time. Rome would eventually free itself of this domination, however, by slowly welcoming Etruscan traditions into its own to make Roman

culture more powerful and then using this
newfound power to finally cast off the Etruscan
hold.

THE RELIGIOSITY OF THE NEW ROME

Romans had a realistic attitude when it came to religious matters. That's probably the reason why they always found it difficult to understand the logic behind worshipping a single, omnipresent, omnipotent god. Romans had their own religion, which was certainly not based on any particular central theme. It was rather a mélange of superstitions, rituals, traditions, and taboos, which they had gathered or learnt from various sources over many years. For Romans, religion was more of a contractual relationship between god-like forces and mankind than a spiritual one. What's more, they believed it to control a human being's well-being and existence. As an example, they kept the Etruscan tradition of making predictions by analyzing the livers of sacrificed animals.

Most of the Romans goddesses and gods resulted from the influence of various regional religions. Some were introduced through the Greek colonies, while some of them had their roots deep in old religions of the Latin tribes. The union of the tribes also led to a new religious union. When the tribes merged, they chose Jupiter and Mars as their protective gods. On the Capitoline they used to worship these two gods, while on the Quirinal, the god Quirinus was also worshipped. The fire of the city was burning continuously in the temple of Vesta, the goddess of family – an institution much respected by the Romans and all the Latins. The Romans were profoundly religious, as their power was thought to come from the gods. From the power of the king to the power of the last, most humble pleasant, everything trickled down from the gods, whether it manifested in peace or war. There was a committee which revealed the festival schedule, as the gods needed to be worshipped and celebrated during lavish festivals.

All of this incorporated religion into the State in a way that is unfamiliar to much of the modern world. The festivals conducted on a regular basis were overseen by religious officials who were employees of the State. The festivals were public rites, and all citizens of Rome were under orders to stop whatever they were doing on these days.

Attendance was not mandatory, but no business could operate on a festival day. This moratorium on work was relatively strict and even extended to slaves who were expected to be afforded at least a modicum of rest. On farms where labor could not stop for even a day, the sacrifice of an animal, such as a pig or a puppy (yes, a puppy!) was sometimes performed as penance. This penance, or "piaculum" could be performed by anyone who needed to work during a religious festival. Individuals could also pay fees to excuse their work. Any work for the gods was permitted, as was work done by doctors of the time if a patient's life was on the line. Perhaps the strongest prohibition surrounded the flamens and the Rex sarcorum who were in charge of the religious rites; these individuals were prohibited from even seeing work during festivals.

This might seem strange to the modern reader, but this approach is easier to understand when one realizes that Rome did not have regular "rest" days the way we do today; in other words, there was no weekend. Regular religious festivals were the only way in which the populace could rest from their labors. At the height of the Republic, the annual calendar was filled to the brim with regular festivals. Any given month in the year might have as many as 8 or 10 festivals. The New Year began with March, which was entirely dedicated to Mars, the warrior god. Then there were sowing festivals dedicated to the gods which protected the harvest and the farmers, as the agricultural year came into full rights. The number of festivals would wane by the end of the Republic, but for a time festivals were the most important and frequent feature of Roman life.

40

PUBLIC VS. PRIVATE FESTIVALS

Compounding the already complex calendar of festivals was the fact that private individuals could also host their own festivals. Public festivals could involve anything from games to religious rites, but wealthy individuals often hosted their own games or "ludi". These events were typically hosted in honor of prominent individuals or families. Neighbors, friends, and important political allies were invited, and these events were often opportunities for wealthy Romans to curry political favor.

Public festivals generally fell into one of four categories: stativae, conceptivae, and imperativae. Stativae were annual events that occurred on a set date. They were typically "national" holidays and observed by everyone. Conceptivae were also held on a yearly basis, but the dates depended on the decision of whichever religious official was overseeing the rites. These so-called "moveable" feasts included

Looking at the various moveable feasts in detail can provide some unique insights into Roman culture at the time. One of the most important of these feasts was the Compitalia. This is perhaps the most ancient of the Ludi stemming back to well before the foundation of Rome. This annual festival was held in honor of the household gods of the crossroads. In the overly mythological telling of later Roman historians, this festival is attributed to Tarquinius Priscus, who is said to have established it after witnessing the miraculous birth of the seventh king of Rome, Servius Tullius.

During this annual festival, families would offer sacrifices at the spot where two roads met. Sacrifices included cakes made from honey. Families hung statues of the goddess of the underworld, Mania, on their doorways, along with wool figures representing men and women. Slaves played a prominent role in the ceremony, perhaps explaining the connection to Servius Tullius, who was rumored to have been born of household slaves. Slaves on this day were afforded complete freedom and rest from their labors according to some historians.

The Sementivae was a fertility festival held several weeks after the Compitalia. This festival of sowing was held each year in honor of the god Tellus and the goddess Ceres. Religious officials carefully timed this moveable feast to ensure that the celebration had the greatest impact on the crops to come in the spring.

Mid-Februrary in Rome brought with it a baking feast for each of the curiae, known as the Fornicalia. The curio maximus would assign a specific date for each curia on which to celebrate its own Fornacaiia, while a single Fornacalia was held for the entire city. This large-scale Fornicalia was for any Roman citizen who may have missed their own curia's festival or else did not have a curia affiliation.

It is assumed by many historians that the Fornicalia was followed shortly by the Amburbium, the cleansing of the city. This purification ceremony is believed by some historians to be the result of a calendar adjustment made by the second of the Roman kings. The Amburbium involved a procession through the city during which chants were sung. Large animals, including bulls and sheep, were also likely sacrificed as part of the ceremony.

Finally, Imperativae were festivals that were held on the order of an official. These rites were typically held in honor of a special event such as a battle, for example, or a particularly important turning point in a prominent Roman's life.

In addition to the religious festivals, Rome also hosted trade fairs on occasion after or in tandem with certain ludi. Known as a mercatus, this commerce fair was meant to encourage trade and boost the economy whenever a large number of citizens had gathered for a festival. These events would become larger, more professional, and more commercial as the trade culture and merchant culture of Rome evolved over time. Popular mercatus fairs that exist in the extant records of Rome include the Mercatus Romani held at the end of September, the Mercatus Apllinares held in July, and the Mercatus Plebeii held in late November.

The tribes already had family gods to worship, and they also added nature gods to this collection in time. The Romans saw gods in every natural event, from a simple rain to a sunny day. In the early days of Rome, when the majority of the people were farmers who depended on the weather and their animals, the number of gods dedicated to the earth and farming was pretty impressive. Jupiter or Jove was the god of the sky and weather phenomena, Tellus was the goddess of the Earth and all the living creatures, Minerva was the goddess of olives, Saturn was the god of sowing, Ceres was the goddess of the harvest, and Flora was the goddess of flowers. There was also Liber, the god of wine, who was just as appreciated then as he is in some ways today. Cheers!

Back to the main three gods of the new Rome—Jupiter, Mars and Quirinus. A special priest, known as a flamen, was assigned to each of these three, central gods. The fire of Vesta was cared for by six virgins, called the vestals, which had a sort of religious immunity. Warriors were prohibited from touching them or harming them in any possible way. Even the king himself with all his power was prohibited from doing so, since the vestals were the daughters of the state and the goddess Vesta. A pontifex maximus was in charge of the religious festivals and the fetiales were trusted to declare war.

Religion played an important part in the life of early Romans, so they often looked up to gods and asked them for favors. Along with prayers, the Romans used to offer their gods certain things, such as flowers and fruits. Honey was another popular pick as a religious gift, and when a person or the entire community had a more serious, larger request to make of a god, an animal was sacrificed for the gods. Sheep, swine, and oxen were the animals typically chosen to carry the Roman's demands to the gods.

IV

THE ROMAN GOVERNMENT

After the first two tribes united in early Rome, they had one more problem to solve: they each had a specific social structure and government. Each of the two tribes came with its own king, a council of elders, and a supportive government structure. But the Palatine tribe and the Quirinal tribe had to merge, so they came up with a new structure. The two kings lost their status and were replaced by one king elected alternately from each tribe. The councils, which counted 100 members, were just united, so they now had a larger council, with 200 members.

Each tribe also had curiae and there were ten members in each tribe. These curiae united as well, so the new Rome had an assembly of 20 curiae.

By the time the third tribe merged into the new Rome, the king was already elected and the curiae and council grew to 30 and 300 members respectively, representing each of the former tribes.

The Roman king was the person who was supposed to rule and lead all the other people. He was elected by the people in the common assembly and when installed on the throne, he also received the approval of the gods. As a king, he was the chief commander of the military forces, the highest priest and the father of all his people. This status gave him the life and death right over all others, giving him the power to call them to arms, grant them special attributes, and administer laws and oversee justice between two or more parties involved in a conflict.

The Senate or the council of elders only had the power to give advice to the king, who could listen to them or not. Later on, the Senate would become more involved in the process of making laws.

The curiae were people who could bear arms and, as such, were in charge of keeping the new city united. Each person had only one vote and the will of the entire assembly was decided by majority of votes. Because the curiae were involved in electing the king and passing laws, they did hold much of the power in their hands in certain ways, perhaps even more than the king. The king's decisions were not final until they were approved by the curiae, for example. One could say that it was this structure that kept democracy alive in the new Rome, controlling the king's decisions and passing them through the filter of the people's will.

Rome's government at the time by and large could best be described as a direct democracy. This meant that various assembled bodies were used to discuss and legislate. These ranged from Comitia, or assemblies that represented all of the public, such as the Curiate, to Concilium, which were councils limited to a specific subset of the population. This Roman system of governance also leveraged Conventio, or conventions, which served as open forums for discussion and opportunities for politicians to orate. Members of the public without political office could also speak at a Conventio, making it one of the first truly democratic forums in Roman culture.

With that overview in place, now let's take a look at each of these components of Roman government in detail.

THE SENATE

The Senate of the Roman Kingdom was the first rumblings of the political model that would eventually transform the world. While the Senate would not enjoy the full breadth of its power until well into the Republic, its inclusion in Roman government in these early years was significant.

The main role of the Senate at this time was as a counselar body to the king. He could call them together at his will, and they were used as a sounding board for any of the ideas the king was dealing with. The Senate used a debate model much like the Greek model that lives on to this day; these political "conversations" were a good way for the king to flesh out ideas. Ultimately, however, the king had veto power and could toss away any suggestions made by the body. Any "law" that was passed by this earliest version of the Senate was essentially just a decree of the king's and not a true product of democracy.

The Senate of this early Rome typically met in a temple or in a consecrated location that had been blessed by a religious official. It was comprised of the patres who ran the leading families of Rome. In this way, this first attempt at populism and democracy was ultimately an oligarchy.

THE CURIATE

Things were a bit more open and democratic over at the Curiate. This assembly evolved over time during the Roman Kingdom and did not reach the apex of its power until the beginning of the Roman Republic. In these early years of Rome, the Curia stemmed from the various Roman families and were ethnic or genealogical in origin. This would evolve throughout the Roman Kingdom as we will discuss. Like the Senate, the Curiate Assembly served to create and pass laws and serve as an open forum for discussing public issues. The plebeians could take part in the Curiate, but voting was left to the Patriae.

The original and most significant curiae consisted of groups culled from the original three tribes established by Romulus during the foundation of Rome. Each tribe had 10 curiae, resulting in 30 curiae that came together in the comitia curiata. Each curia had its own name. Uniquely, it is rumoured that these names came from the names of the Sabine women abducted by Rome in that legendary story. Curia names that have survived the test of time include Calabra, Faucia, Foriensis, Tifata, and Titia, to name just a few.

Each curia served as a religious group of sorts, with its members worshipping gods unique to their curia in addition to the gods of the Roman state. Every curia had their own temple or place of worship. This site was typically named after the curia itself. In the earliest years of Rome, the place of worship may have been a basic altar, but as the size and power of various curiae grew, these religious sites would become large-scale temples and meeting houses.

Every curia also had its own elected official known as a curio who oversaw all the religious affairs of the group. Elected for life, the curio was typically an elder and over 50 years of age (ancient by Roman estimation). This curio, in turn, worked with a flamen curialis, a religious officer assigned to that curia. When the comitia curiata would convene, all of the various curiones from the curiae answered to a single curio maximus, also an elected official.

The comitia curiata had a range of responsibilities, including electing magistrates, bequeathing priestly sacraments upon individuals, and overseeing wills. By the end of the Roman Kingdom, the power of the comitia curiata would wane as the paradigm for power shifted from ethnic affiliation to land ownership.

THE MANY FACES OF THE ROMAN KING

Let's take a moment now to look more specifically at the multiple roles the king played in the early days of Rome.

One of the king's primary roles was that of the State's Chief Executive, much like the role served by the U.S. President today. In this role, the king held supreme authority over the military and over the judicial system of Rome. This authority was known as the imperium and was bestowed upon the monarch by the Comitia Curiata. In this way, the will of the people was closely tied to the rule of the king. The king's authority over the military in particular, however, was all but supreme.

The king as Chief Executive was also tasked with appointing individuals to all the key appointments throughout the Roman kingdom. One of the most essential was his own tribune, or tribunus celerum, who served as his right-hand man, convened the Curiate, and helped form legislation. This role could be seen as similar to today's Vice President or even the Speaker of the U.S. House of Representatives. The king also chose the man who would serve as the warden of Rome, the praefectus urbi. If a war campaign took the king out of the city, the warden was left in charge, with all the powers of the king in his hands.

A second but culturally as relevant role for the king was that of Rome's Chief Priest. He was the ultimate advocate for the people to the gods and the bridge between the common people and the dieties. He was, in essence, Rome's primary seer and the ultimate authority when it came to religious matters. In many ways, this role can be seen as the predecessor by several centuries of the Roman pope. The king's role as the main voice of the Gods in Roman life allowed him to carefully shape the lives of Romans and the culture of the city, setting major holidays, telling the people which Gods to worship, and creating an overall tenor to the religion of Rome.

Finally, the King also served as the Chief Legislator and Judge of Rome. With respect to his role as Legislator, he ruled with a heavy hand over the Senate and Curiate, who had limited independence. While the Senate would achieve supremacy later during the Republic, during this time it was still at the beck and call of the King. It was a mere demonstration of democracy, in other words, rather than active democracy. What's more, as we shall see in the sections to come, Rome at this point was still very much a timocracy; as such, power in the political structure laid primarily in the hands of the rich. Needless to say, the King called and dismissed these assemblies whenever he chose, relying on them only to approve a formal declaration of war against a neighboring tribe.

In his role as the Chief Judge, the King of Rome had final say on every case heard within the confines of Rome. The King oversaw trials in both criminal and civil matters, advised by a small council. This court system also included the Quaestores Parricidi who investigated cases for the King a two-man team that handled cases of treason. There is some disagreement amongst historians as to whether the King's decisions were final. Some historians believe that his decisions could on occasion be appealed through the Curiate, but a patrician was needed to file the appeal in the first place.

ELECTION

While the Senate was "decorative" in many ways during the time of the Roman Kingdom, they did wield a good deal of power when it came to the election of the king. The death of a king started a period known as the "interregnum"—literally "between kings". All powers typically bestowed on the king transferred during this time to the Senate. The Senate was also in charge of selecting the new King by way of election. During this election process, an Interrex or "in-between king", if you will, took on the mantle of king. This title transferred from one senator to the next every five days until a suitable replacement was found. The Senate would then review the nominee in detail and run a up-down vote on his ascension to the throne. Much like in the modern U.S. Congress, the nominee would need to pass through one body before being transferred to the next body for a second election. In other words, a nominee who cleared the Roman Senate then went through a vote at the Curiate. Finally, the people of Rome had the authority to reject a nominee, while an augur would also need to confer with the auspices to determine whether the new nominee had the favor of the gods. At the end of this complex process, the Senate would then bestow the power of the imperium onto the king-elect in a ceremony. While tinged with religious overtones, it is easy to see how this process was the predecessor in many ways of the modern electoral system.

THE CONSTITUTION OF THE ROMAN KINGDOM

What constituted the Constitution of the Roman Kingdom consisted of a set of unwritten rules that guided to political operations of the city. It is believed that these guidelines were agreed to through precedent and experience, essentially building the system "by ear" as the Romans went along. The main principles of the Constitution defined the powers of the King and the Senate as discussed in the previous sections. The king might call the Senate or the Curiate Assembly to order and request that they take a vote on various issues, but he was free to disregard that vote if he deemed it necessary. The main function of these assemblies under the Constitution, given this ultimate authority of the king, was to serve as a forum for the concerns of the public and the patriae.

The evolution of the Constitution of the Roman Kingdom can be used to divide this historical period into two eras. We will look at each king in detail in the following chapter, but for now it suffices to discuss their reigns within the frameworks of these two eras.

The first era, the legendary epoch that covered what is believed to be the reign of the first four kings, involved building the initial foundation of this Constitution. The religious rites of the kingdom were established, the population of Rome was separated into the various curiae, and the Senate and Curiate were formed into official institutions. As the population of Rome swelled due to various conquests, the people of Rome were divided into ethnic groups. These groups—the Ramnes, the Tities, and the Luceres—incorporated the Latins, Sabines, and Etruscans respectively into the Roman population. The earliest patrician families stemmed from each of these categories, later defining the curiae. Two, main assemblies evolved from these divisions—the Curiate Assembly and the Calate Assembly, each of which answered the needs of specific ethnic groups within the Roman populace. The town elders who had originally served as the aristocracy of earliest Rome would also evolve into the Senate at this time.

The second Constitutional era of the Roman Kingdom covered the reigns of the last three of the seven kings. The reigns of these kings were defined by wide-ranging conquests that spread the reach of Rome much further than it had ever been. This also translated into more and more (and more diverse) people entering the Roman populace. These people at first fell under the protection of various patrician families, but as their power grew in Rome, they began to break off into the plebian class. This created a unique catch-22 for Rome—as plebians were released from their curiae, they were also released from their military obligations. As the Roman army had to remain well-manned, the patrician families found themselves essentially negotiating with the plebeians, requesting that they return to the curiae and serve. This wound eventually culminate into a high-stakes conflict between the plebeians and the patricians—a conflict that would define much of the Republican era.

During the Roman Kingdom, however, the powers that be found some unique ways to bring the plebeians back into the military fold. One of the later kings, Servius Tullius, swapped out the hereditary model that defined the curiae and replaced it with one based solely on land ownership. This game-changing pivot transformed Roman society and the Constitution as it had existed until then. Plebeians could now find affiliation and a modicum of political power through membership in this new Century Assembly. In contrast, tribal affiliations also saw an uptick at this time ironically. All of Rome essentially divided into four tribes, although access to these affiliations was open to both patricians and plebes and therefore much more flexible than the original system.

V

THE LEGENDARY TALE OF THE SEVEN KINGS

As the saying goes, history is always written by the winners. The story of the beginning of Rome is no different. It may have been warped by legends and made up of fabled stories, but it seems only natural to paint the past of an empire as extravagant as Rome with such a colorful and broad brush.

However, it would not be correct to say that these accounts are mere rhetoric. From these stories, we learn how spirited the Roman people were and how their customs and traditions originated. While some stories may seem too opulent to be true, there are certainly some that form an important part of the world's historical literature.

One such story is the one that defines the rule of the seven kings of Rome. Discussing these noteworthy kings can give us insight into the socio-political system that they disseminated in their respective reigns.

THE HISTORICAL RECORD OF THE REGAL ERA

Tracing the historical record of the Regal Era in Rome is a difficult task, primarily due to the fact that there was no written record kept of the period at the time. The first written records recounting the period from 753 to 509 B.C. do not appear until centuries later. In the years before the Christian Era, Greek historians were the primary authorities on regional history. Rome, essentially, did not even appear on their "radar" until the Pyrrhic War, which took place nearly 500 years after the establishment of Rome.

Rome itself did not gain its own historian of note until around 200 B.C., when the senator Quintus Fabius Pictor began documenting his city's story. It is important to note that Pictor drafted much of his history of Rome from the perspective of victor; after all, he lived in a time when Rome had already captured much of the Italian peninsula and moved on to wage war against Carthage. For this reason, Pictor's perspective on Roman history is often heroic and perhaps a bit skewed. His approach to the historical record would define the work of Roman historians for years to come, establishing what is now known as the "annalistic" tradition and tracks Rome from year to year.

Arguably the most prominent historian from this tradition was Livy, who followed Quintus Fabius Pictor nearly two hundred years later. It is from Livy's writings that modern historians glean much of what they know about the earliest years of Rome. His work and the work of historians like him was difficult. They had a barebones framework from which to flesh out their historical records. From the Republic onward, there were religious records and annual documentation from the consular fasti that could provide an outline to historical events. To flesh out these events and for any of the events in the earliest years of Rome, historians often turn to regional legends and even Greek mythology.

As such and as we discussed earlier, much of what we know from this period is a unique combination of fact and fiction. Since it was written from the perspective of the victor, it also involves a good bit of self-aggrandizement. These stories from the earliest years, therefore, can be instructive, but should also be taken with a grain or two of salt.

Much of this strange combination of fact and legend is evident in the narrative of the Seven Kings of Rome. Some, such as the first king, Romulus, may stem completely from legend, while others ring more true. In all of these stories sounds the need of the later Roman historians to consolidate the historical record and establish a legendary past for the city state and burgeoning Empire. Roman historians used these stories to explain existing customs, institutions, and traditions and establish the myth-like reputation of Rome.

THE ARCHAEOLOGICAL RECORD

Using the archaeological record to confirm or deny the historical record is problematic in the Mediterranean region. As happens often in Greece, much of what was Rome is now covered by what is Rome, making excavations difficult. What is known about the earliest years of Rome is that the first settlement was located on the Palatine Hill and that the growing town eventually expanded to the Esquiline Hill. These facts actually contradict the written stories, which claim that the Quirinal Hill was the second settlement in early Rome. By the 7th century B.C., the settlements had extended down into the valley between the hills. Here, the early Romans began to enjoy life in more solidly built abodes with stone foundations and experienced a quality of life on par with vibrant artisan communities of the time. By the time of Rome's last kings, this small town had been transformed into a city with a public center, public works, and a thriving trade.

THE PRESUMPTIVE TIMELINE OF THE KINGS

Solid dates are not known for any of the kings, of course, due to the fable-like quality of the historical record. There are general assumptions made based on the works of later Roman historians. To get an idea of the time period incorporated by the reign of the seven kings, you can use the following table as a general reference. I have also included general characteristics of each reign to give you an initial overview of each ruler.

Year	King	Characteristics
753–717 BC	Romulus	Foundation of Rome; mythological ties to Ancient Troy
716–673 BC	Numa Pompilius	The first creation of major religious institutions in Rome

Year	King	Characteristics
673–642 BC	Tullus Hostilius	The conquest of Alba Longa and the incorporation of the Albans into the citizenry of Rome
640–616 BC	Ancus Marcius	Ongoing conflicts with neighboring tribes, including the Sabines and Albans
616–579 BC	Tarquin the Elder	Consolidated growing citizenry into larger Senate; built the Circus Maximus
578–535 BC	Servius Tullius	Established the first coinage for Rome and the census
535–509 BC	Tarquin the Proud	Last king of Rome; considered the pinnacle of tyranny by some, leading to the Republic

From this initial chart, you can get an idea of the momentum that built throughout the period of Kings in Rome. From its humble beginnings a basic, agrarian settlement on a hill, Rome would grow during this time to include some of the most complex and rich social systems of the day. On that note, let us now dive in to the tale of each of the Roman kings in greater detail.

THE FIRST KING - ROMULUS

The first king of Rome was Romulus, one of the twins of Rhea Silvia and a descendant of the royal family of Alba Longa. The foundation of the senate is attributed to him. He is in fact known to have brutally adopted the policy of expanding the empire and accepting the criminals from the asylum on Capitoline Hill. He established a city state in the name of Rome, and is also considered the father of all social and political systems in the civilization.

A central problem facing the early reign of Romulus was that his city state was composed almost entirely of refugees, runaway slaves, and criminals, with a serious shortage of women. In order to create families, he undertook what is still remembered as one of the most underhanded moments in the history of the Western world, abducting the Sabine women. It is known as the "Rape of the Sabine Women", although the verb used more directly translates as "abduction". However one parses the language, this turning point in Roman history is so iconic that it has appeared in countless works of art as late as the 20th century.

How Romulus got away with this tumultuous act is a thing of legend. The story goes that he hosted an extravagant series of celebrations around the festival of Consus, a god of the storehouse and an essential figure in those hungry, early years. Romulus invited all of the local tribes to the events, including many Sabines. In the middle of the elaborate celebration, it is said Romulus stopped everything and revealed his true intention in inviting the guests—he planned on keeping the Sabine women in his realm and marrying them off to his men. He himself would take a wife, as well, a woman named Hersilia.

It may come as no surprise that the Sabines did not take too kindly to this turn of events. King Titus Tatius, the leader of the nearby Sabine town of Cures, declared open war on Rome and Romulus, leading to the battle for the Capitoline Hill. In this epic battle, the Roman Tarpeia betrayed his city by opening the gates to the Sabine warriors. To this day, the Tarpeian Rock on the Capitoline Hill marks this treacherous act. Records are sparse as to how this battle was reconciled—one popular story claims that the abducted Sabine women themselves stopped the battle and brought peace between the Sabine men and the Romans.

However peace was attained, this stalemate would remain in place for the duration of Romulus' 37-year reign. The peace agreed to by both sides placed Titus Tatius as ruler on the Capitoline, while Romulus ruled from the Palatine. When the Sabine king passed away, Romulus ruled both kingdoms peaceably for the rest of his life.

While the historical record from this period is rife with legend, there are historical truths that point to the veracity of these accounts, at least supporting the notion that the union between Sabines and Romans did take place. Perhaps the way in that the union occurred was not through confrontation or abduction, but through agreement. The Romans would continue, for example, to use the name "quirite" to refer to themselves on occasion, a word derived from the Sabine version of the Roman god Mars. However verifiable these stories may be, they resonate with the true tenor of Rome and make for compelling history.

THE DEATH OF ROMULUS

Romulus death is still under the shroud of myth. The driving narrative combines fable and truth, stating that while he was performing rituals to the God by the river side, a thunderstorm struck. While the citizens of Rome ran away to protect themselves, Romulus was left behind with senators; when they returned, Romulus was not to be found anywhere. Legend says that he must have been swept by his father Mars into the heavens while performing that ritual sacrifice to the gods by the river. What is closer to the truth and what most historians say is that Romulus had grown so unpopular that his senators stabbed him to his death to end his reign of tyranny.

Around this time, there was no system of succession by hierarchy; kings were selected from amongst the people. Choosing a successor was complicated by the controversy around Romulus' death. Just after his death, the leading senator at the time claimed that he saw Romulus in a dream and that the dead king was now a God. This absolved the senators of all assumed wrong doings and made way for one Julius Proculus to become the next king. The Roman people, however, were not very happy with this decision, which made the king's possible murderer his successor, and demanded that one of the Sabines instead be made king. The choice was Numa Pompilius, a man who didn't even want the throne since, unlike Romulus, he was not a warrior but a cultural and religious person. In one of the great ironies of early Rome, therefore, a violent king brought down by violence led to a peace-loving, art-appreciating and spiritual man in Numa Pompilius.

THE SECOND KING – NUMA POMPILIUS

The death of Romulus resulted in an interregnum period that ran as long as a year, leaving Rome to be ruled by a different senator every five days for the entire year. This delay was primarily due to the infighting between the Roman factions and the Sabine factions in the senate. As a compromise and when it seemed that the interregnum might go on forever, the roman faction ceded to Sabine will and granted the throne to Numa Pompilius, a Sabine.

Famed Roman historian, Plutarch, described this king as a cunning person. This ability to play people may have been evident in these very first moments as king, as Numa Pompilius at first actually turned down the role. It took the cajoling of his father and a host of kinsmen along with an embassy from Rome to persuade him to take the throne. Before ascending, he requested that one of Rome's augurs consult with the gods to confirm that he should be in power. Perhaps this faux humility was the easiest way to slip into the role without alienating the Roman faction and was cannily done.

Upon taking the throne, Numa is said to have disbanded the king's royal guard. This may have been yet another gesture of humility or it may have been done out of a need to get allies of the Roman faction away from his person.

He is believed to have established the Roman calendar and created national borders, dividing the lands for the sake of the people and propagating religion. For this reason, he is also considered by many to be the father of Roman religion. He was known to be quite ascetic, eschewing all luxuries and forbidding any indulgence or decadence in his home. Some, including Plutarch himself, hint at this piety as yet another ruse, claiming that he was yet again cannily positioning himself as divine in order to inspire less warlike behavior from the Roman faction. Whatever his motivations, Numa had a significant influence on Roman religion.

This king drafted several sacred books which he claimed were divine and passed down from the Muses. These books are assumed to have included many of the rites built around the priesthood of Rome, covering flamines, fetiales, and rituals. It is said that, at his death, Numa asked to be buried with the only versions of these books so that the traditions would go on as living practices and not stagnate in the written word.

All in, Numa Pompilius is said to have restored civility amongst the barbaric Romans while he was on the throne. Numa is known to have reformed the Roman calendar as he added two new months – January and February – and brought the total number of days to a count of 360 for each year. Rome enjoyed complete, uninterrupted peace during the 43 years of his reign. Numa, to Romans, was the father of Roman culture. He was indeed the man who led a pile of criminals, semi-barbarian peasants, and robbers into a new culture of civility.

THE THIRD KING – TULLUS HOSTILIUS

After the death of this calm and religious king, the pendulum swung back once again to a warlike figure. Chosen from the Romans, Tullus Hostilius was the third king to reign over the empire. In his early days, many disputes arose from petty issues, such as cattle rustling. While Numa had been a diplomatic figure who always hoped to gain reconciliation, his successor, Tullus Hostilius, was the kind of person who defaulted to resolving issues by the power of his sword.

His period of influence was marked by the complete subjugation of Alba Longa. When Tullus declared war on Alba Longa, he wanted to avoid the slaughtering of armies that were related to one another, given the close ties between the two cities. Instead, the two leaders from both the sides agreed on a trial by combat. In place of an army, three brothers from each side would fight, representing their respective cities. Horatians volunteered for the Romans while Curiatius fought for the Albans. When the fight ended, one of the Horatii remained alive, making the Romans the victors. Alba Longa had to accept defeat and swear their allegiance to Rome.

Alba Longa, however, did not truly accept defeat and provoked another province into a battle with Rome. Alba Longa's King Mettius turned to the Fidenates and encouraged them to challenge Rome. Rome headed into battle with the Albans by their side, oblivious to the fact that they were moments away from being betrayed. Once the Albans switched sides, Rome managed to defeat the Fidenates nonetheless. The powerful Roman army then turned on the Ablans, and they were singlehandedly defeated by the Romans, their city later razed to the ground. The surviving Albans were moved to Rome where they inhabited the Caelian Hill.

This rapid influx of new citizens took a toll on Rome's senate, where space was limited. Ironically, this betrayal therefore led to one of Tullus' greatest accomplishments—the construction of the Curia Hostilia at the western end of the Forum.

Tullus continued his war campaigns around the region, also expanding his influence to the neighboring Sabine tribes. Tullus likely would have continued for years in this combative mode if a plague had not come to victimize his people. Seeing this as a sign of the gods' wrath towards his militaristic behavior, Tullus attempted to curry the gods' favor. To avert their wrath, Tullus began taking his religious duties more seriously and abstained from war. This switch did not fare well for Tullus, however, and fate had other plans for him. At the height of his new piety, he was struck by lightning and died.

While Tullus' legacy left him with mixed reviews, his war campaigns did benefit Rome in the long run. The absorption of the Albans into the Roman population brought new complexity and prestige to Rome and made it an even more culturally rich city than before.

THE FOURTH KING – ANCUS MARSICUS

The fourth king of Rome was Numa Pompilius' grandson Ancus Marsicus, which meant another Sabine would rule the empire. Romans chose him as their next king so that peace could be restored and they could enjoy the calmness that they experienced under the rule of Numa. According to Roman historians, Ancus Marsicus was another great king who brought prosperity to the Roman Empire through his military efficiency. He brought back many of his grandfather's laws and worked toward the cultural development of the city of Rome. He built bridges and ports and secured the nation with many forts and towers.

Unfortunately, it is said that Ancus Marsicus' piety made some of his neighbors think him an easy target. The Old Latins, a neighboring tribe with ancient origins, tried their hand at testing his mettle. Luckily for Rome, Ancus Marsicus was not found wanting when it came to military might, and he handily defeated the Old Latins. All of his military conquests are of special note. From his conquest over the Old Latins, which it is said led to the razing of their city and the absorption of their population into Rome, it is believed to have resulted in the expansion of Rome to the Aventine Hill.

Other successes of Ancus Marsicus' reign include the founding of the city of Ostia, at least according to legend. The archaeological record suggests that the city was founded at a somewhat later date. Ancus Marsicus is also credited with putting up the first bridge over the Tiber river and creating a bridgehead at the Janiculan Hill. This strategic choice created a fortification against the Etruscans and offered protection to a key trade route along the western edge of the river.

Long after his death, he was still respected by his subjects. Ancus Marsicus was not only an excellent warrior but also a great administrator, diplomat, and priest. Later generations of his family, the Marcii, were allowed into the consulship, cementing the legitimacy of these semi-mythical king.

THE FIFTH KING – LUCIUS TARQUINIUS PRISCUS

The fifth king to come into power was Lucius Tarquinius Priscus. Tarquin, also known as the 'The Elder", is said to have moved to Rome from Tarquinii, an Estruscan town. His father was a noble man who belonged to Corinth and was asked to depart from the city when Cypselus came to power. If the legend is to be believed, when Tarquin was about to enter Rome, an eagle snatched his cap with its talons and placed it on his head again, proving that this man has been chosen by providence to rule over Rome.

To organically fit into Roman nobility, he changed his name from Lucomo to Lucius. Soon he married Tanaquil, a woman belonging to Etruscan aristocracy. In no time, Tarquin rose in the ranks and became an influential figure in Rome. He further expanded his range of influence to the then reigning king, Ancus Marcicus, becoming one of his trusted advisors and the guardian of his two sons. Tarquin usurped the throne when the king died and sent the sons away on the pretext of performing the dead king's last rites. In their absence, he won over the hearts of Romans, and they elected him as their next king. Since the Roman monarchy was not based on heredity, it was easy for Tarquin to use his charisma to his advantage and take over the throne. Although his way of taking over the throne might not have been that impressive, the way he managed the kingdom as a monarch was very much so. He had to bid goodbye to all the challenges related to military of the neighboring tribes, which threatened his position as monarch. Instead, he took on infrastructure improvements throughout Rome. Tarquin the Elder is credited by some with building the Temple of Jupiter Capitolinus, as well as introducing the Circus Games to the city. Legend says that he also created both the Circus Maximus and the Cloaca Maxima and introduced 100 new minors gentes to the Senate from local Etruscan tribes. All of this secured his authority, strengthened ties throughout the region, and improved the quality of life for Romans.

Despite these efforts, Tarquin was still destined for a warrior's death. King Ancus' sons would return to wreak their revenge on Tarquin the Elder, murdering him in a bloody confrontation with an axe. Tarquin's wife would step up in this moment and begin pulling the strings that would lead to the succession of the next king. While Tarquin was killed instantly by the brothers' attack. Tanaquil put out that the king was still alive and suggested that one of Tarquin's son-in-law's henchman, the wily and savvy Servius Tullius, make decisions in his stead while the king recovered. This bit of subterfuge succeeded leading to the sixth and perhaps most impressive King of Rome.

THE SIXTH KING – SERVIUS TULLIUS

The sixth king to assume leadership of the Roman Empire, Servius Tullius, is highly celebrated by historians for his achievements. The origins of Servius are not clear, but his name seems to be a corrupt derivation of the word "servus" meaning slave. He is known to have been the successor of a slave in the royal family; someone who was favored by the gods.

As referenced above, his ascension to the throne is said to have been the doing of Talaquin, wife of Tarquinius Priscus. The powerful queen of the king believed that Servius had special abilities that were compatible with someone worthy of being a king. She secretly helped him get on the throne after the death of Tarquin and manipulated the citizens of Rome into giving him the throne.

Talaquin's faith in this man was proven right when Rome went to war against Veii. Servius Tullius proved himself to be a worthy successor to Tarquin. His victory was so impressive, in fact, that, in the 44 years of his reign that followed, Rome never had to take to the battlefield again.

Servius Tullius' successes within the city of Rome were just as dramatic. He is believed to have created the large, earthenwork defenses around several hills of Rome as well as the Servian Wall. He also expanded the boundaries of the city, it is thought, to accommodate Rome's growing population. He is also credited with completing construction on the Temple of Jupiter started by his predecessor.

He was an innovator as well. He was the first king to use a coinage system in the city. He introduced metal coins to replace the old barter system, allowing the first, primitive monetary system to evolve during his rule. In perhaps his most important achievement, he also introduced the census, which counted people in his territory and classified them according to wealth. This created increased tax revenue for Rome, providing him with the funds for his infrastructure projects and giving him the ability to grow the military. Servius Tullus also gave the ever-expanding military its own political assembly, known as the comitia centuriata.

Tullus didn't stop there. Additional achievements include a treaty signed with the Latins which established Rome as the head of this pivotal, regional tribe and the construction of the Temple to Diana on the Aventine Hill.

As with many an ancient king, Tullus Servius' epic efforts in the service of Rome meant nothing in the end. He was to find a bloody end like many kings of old, in this case at the hands of his own daughter Tullia, and her husband Lucius Tarquin. The stories that have come down from this time tell us that these two led a coup against Tullus at the end of his reign, with his own son-in-law murdering him and ascending to the throne as seventh and last king of Rome, Tarquin the Proud.

THE SEVENTH KING – TARQUIN THE PROUD

The final and 7th king to reign over the ancient Roman Empire was Tarquin 'The Proud' or the son/grandson of Tarquin 'the Elder'. His ascension to the throne is marked by conspiracy, according to the legends. Also according to tradition, he is remembered as a cruel despot. Since he was did not have a legitimate claim to the throne, he used trickery to gain control of the empire. He took over the throne as the last king by murdering his father-in-law, grabbing power without even the consent of the people or the senate. He coveted both fame and power. He is known to be one of the most violent and oppressive kings in the history of Rome.

Historians, however, add that even though he was a tyrannical king, his performance as a diplomat and as a military commander was rather impressive. He played a huge role in increasing the military power of Rome. His diplomatic acumen helped him talk the Latin into treating Rome as their official head and made them sign the Treaty of Ferentia. As a result he not only strengthened the military power of Rome but also brought a key ally to Rome's side. The spoils that he received from his conquests were used in public works like building and improving the roads, intensifying Rome's defenses etc.

Despite all of this, Rome was seething with resentment, as their king continued to rob the rich and exploit the poor. This continued oppression gave birth to an uprising which eventually failed as the king was fighting yet another military campaign. The straw that finally broke the camel's back was when a noblewoman Lucretia was raped by Tarquin's son. The city went into an uproar. At long last, the oppressive king was overthrown and Rome was declared a republic. The Roman monarchy had fallen into disrepute and the city became a res publica for the people.

All these Estruscan Kings were known to be powerful figures and they definitely contributed to the dominance of Rome. As we have seen, their incredible power was initially used for the people's good but later turned into brutal and hateful tyranny. Their contribution towards giving Rome a certain kind of influence and strength was marvelous, and in many ways they transformed the character and the will of the people of Rome. Needless to say, much of Roman history has to be written about and discussed with a pinch of salt. Even though much of the narrative around these seven kings contains myth and legend, there are also kernels of truth that make it all the more interesting. It may be hard to tell the truth from a fable, but there is no one who can deny the glory of the Roman Empire.

VI

TRANSITION FROM ROMAN KINGDOM TO THE ROMAN REPUBLIC

With each subsequent ruler of Rome, the sense of power each ruler felt increased exponentially. They were not just rulers but also eventually tyrants in the lives of the common people. To make things worse, it was not just the rulers but also their family members who behaved in an inappropriate manner, sometimes being so downright malicious and loathsome that people slowly started feeling more angst than respect and loyalty towards those who led the nation. The incident that shook the pillars of the royalty in Rome so badly that the whole institution or governance had to come crashing down was the rape of one of the most prominent women in Rome.

The transition of Rome from a Kingdom to a Republic was an outcome of a political revolution in around 509 BC. This revolution in ancient Rome put an end to the Roman Monarchy and led to the establishment of the Roman Republic. According to history, while Lucius Tarquinius Superbus, the last Etruscan king, was out on a campaign, his son raped a woman named Lucretia. Lucretia was a legendry noble woman who then committed suicide after revealing this bitter truth to some of the noblemen. These Roman men, in turn, with the help of aristocracy, got the king expelled, which marked the end of the kingdom. This incident invoked a feeling of hatred among the people and they started displaying open dissatisfaction towards the rule of Lucius. The prominent people started driving away the royal family and instituting a republic. They were successful in forming their Republic and protected it against the Etruscan.

They enlisted an army, and Rome's gates were blocked by these new soldiers. There were general elections held and the vote went to the Republic, effectively putting the monarchy to an end.

People were fed up of being ill-treated by their rulers. But this incident acted like an incendiary force and set afire the need for justice, retribution, and freedom from the oppression that people in all parts of Rome were suffering from. In order to understand the incident, let us first look at the people who were involved in it and understand what their position and relation to each other was.

As mentioned earlier, the last king of Rome, Lucius Tarquinius Superbus, was busy waging a war at Ardea. In order to attend to some military needs in Collatia, he sent his son Sextus Tarquinius in his stead to this place, which was governed by Lucius Tarquinius Collatinus. Collatinus was in fact related to the last king Superbus; he was the king's nephew, Arruns Tarquinius' son, who was also a governor of Collatia and was in fact the first of the Tarquinii Collatini to be so. Coming back to the present governor Collatinus – he was married to Lucretia, who was the daughter of a very popular and highly esteemed man in Rome, Spurius Lucretius. It was perhaps her unique position of power, her association with integrity from her childhood, and the honor and bravery of her husband which gave her the ability to take a very drastic step when her honor was damaged by none other than the son of King Superbus – Sextus Tarquinius.

There are many versions of this story but they all more or less converge on a few facts. The core of the story is that Lucretia's modesty was severely outraged; her body was invaded without her consent and she was assaulted by Sextus. Lucretia was at home when she received the king's son in their house as a guest because he, instead of his father, had visited her town to take care of some military matters. It was said that she was a quiet, beautiful, and totally reputable soul who was the vision of hospitality itself when she took care of her guests. She knew the importance of doing so, especially since, in one version of the story, her husband too was with King Superbus at the siege in Ardea.

In the most widely accepted version of the story from there on, it is believed that Egerius, Colatinus, and Sextus were having a merry time together by drinking a lot of alcohol and discussing the most meritorious wives in Rome. Each one extolled the virtues of the ladies or wives in their acquaintance, but the playful banter and discussion didn't end here. In order to check whether their claims were true or false, they decided to visit the houses of each one, see what their respective wives were doing and decide who was the most honorable of them all. The exact words used here were "Young and vigorous as we are, why don't we go get our horses and go and see for ourselves what our wives are doing? And we will base out judgement on whatever we see them doing when their husbands arrive unannounced." This was regarded as a splendid idea and each one jumped on to the backs of their horses and raced towards their houses. In the houses of Sextus and Egerius, the women were busy preparing for a feast and for some merry time in the absence of their husbands. Lucretia, wife of Collatinus and our heroine in this chapter, was however doing something totally unexpected at her home – she sat quietly weaving with a few other people in her house. Needless to say, Collatinus was declared the winner of their silly challenge and discussion because his wife was the most virtuous of all the wives involved in the experiment. But the lady who had won this contest, probably completely unaware of the entire story until her last moment, did not know that it was her chaste attitude, her beauty and probably jealousy, that drove Superbus' son Sextus to fall in love with her or obsess about her. The men went to their respective camps for the night; either on the same day, or after the passage of a few days, Sextus made way to Collatinus' house with only one purpose in mind – to take advantage of the beautiful and honorable Lucretia's body and mind.

It is still not very clear from all the recorded texts due to conflicting or varying information as to what Sextus' state of mind was. Some scholars, who wrote those ancient records, understood that Sextus was enamored by Lucretia's beauty while the others think it was a combination of lust and marvel at her chastity that drove Sextus to the house of Collatinus, past all the servants who lay on the floor, to the room where Lucretia lay asleep. Here again one must note that there are different versions about how the rape was carried out and what were the actions after that.

In one version, it is said that Sextus returned to Collatinus's house under the pretext of official duties and carried out the heinous act late in the night. As Lucretia was an honorable woman, he knew she would not agree to have an illicit affair with him unless she was forced to do so. Hence, Sextus carried his sword with him and when he entered her room, he placed his naked sword on her left breast and firstly praised her, expressed his love for her and tried to cajole her to comply with his base wishes. He even agreed to make her king when he ascends the throne but all his attempts were in vain. When she refused, he threatened to kill her and place her naked body beside the naked body of a common servant. He would then prove to the world that she was an adulterous woman and her name would be tainted forever. Poor Lucretia did not want to die such a death and had to submit to rape.

In another version of the story, it is said that Sextus was washing her belly with water when she woke up and felt her body and soul were defiled by this man.

Sextus went his own way after he damaged the innocent body and mind of Lucretia; fortunately, however, Lucretia was surrounded by men of honor, prestige, and bravery. The common version of the story from here on is that she summoned her father and husband on an urgent basis and explained to them the events of the previous night. In order to ensure her story was not disbelieved and dismissed outright, she brought forth a witness who corroborated her claims. When all the people gathered understood the seriousness of the matter, they proceeded to console her and let her know that her mind was as pure and untarnished as before, no matter what Sextus had done with her body. But Lucretia did not want her name to be associated with the misdeed but with honor, and she removed a concealed dagger and stabbed herself to death in front of the men and women there, to prove that she was not lying and that she could not live a life with such a taint. In another version of the story, she herself went to her father's court where her husband and a witness were summoned and she narrated the story of Sextus' misdeeds. But the story again ends on a note of tragedy when she kills herself. In another version of the story, Collatinus and Brutus, a friend of her husband, were returning to Rome when they were informed of this situation and they rushed to her room, only to find her dead.

But at the end of each version, she exacted a promise from her father, her husband, and their friends whom they had brought along as witnessed, Brutus as Collanitus' friend and Publius Valerius Publicola with Lucretia's father, that they would avenge her death and that the person who raped her would be suitably punished.

Now, Brutus was ill-treated by the king and had an additional motive to overthrow the reign of the monarchy. Collanitus was simply overwhelmed and shocked by his wife's honorable, fatal act and could only hold her in her arms, weep and promise to fulfil his last promise made to her. A combination of hate, ambition, and justice overtook the men linked directly or indirectly with Lucretia, and they succeeded in rousing the hatred of the rest of the people in Rome to such an extent that the Royal Family was banished from the kingdom. No further intrusions from the Etruscans and tribal Latins were allowed and the foundations of the Common Era were laid.

People avenged the death of Lucretia by ensuring the powerful men who had defiled her and who had caused so many other miseries were punished, and this converted the Roman Kingdom into a Roman Republic.

There are countless research papers, books, plays, and other forms of data dedicated to this pivotal incident in the history or Rome. It is impossible to study the history of Rome without knowing about this catalyst which spurred the people to hold open courts, debated and secret meetings to overthrow the royalty's rule and bring about the reign of people elected by the people.

Because of all this, the rape incident is known to have played a major role in the Roman literature and art. Lucretia's story is thus not remembered as just another historical story, but also as a legend in the early history.

CONCLUSION

These tumultuous events led to one of the pivotal events in Western Civilization- the establishment of the Roman Republic. This period, which spanned nearly 500 years from 509 B.C. to 27 B.C., saw Rome consolidate its power well beyond the Italian peninsula, expanding its reach throughout the East and into North Africa. Along the way, the Republic would go through diverse phases of development, expanding on the existing bureaucracies and systems to create one of the most complex social systems the world had seen up until that point.

In the next book in this series, we will look at the Rise and eventual demise of the Roman Republic in detail, before transitioning into the Roman Empire itself in Book 3. From here on out we are in more certain territory, as the historical records for this period of time transition from an amalgam of myth and pseudo-fact to more truthful narratives. In discussing the at times mythic pre-history of Rome here, however, I hope you have gotten an idea of the rich complexity that defined Rome and what is to come. It's a story you will not want to miss.

ABOUT THE AUTHOR

Victor Miller is a 45 year old man living in historic Charleston South Carolina with his wife Jackie and two kids Kevin and Mark. Victor is a lover of history. Growing up he loved to learn about the ancient romans, Greeks as well as other historical events.

After completing high school he began to see the world. Taking a trip to Egypt to see the pyramids and then off to Rome and the surrounding areas he was able to see the worlds that he loved first hand. After getting married he began to settle down and began to write about his travels. He would be invited by high schools and other institutions of learning to tell his tales and show off artifacts that he has collected to students and staff.

With the development of Amazon and their publishing platforms Victor has been able to share his writings and love of history with the world. As of 2015 he plans on writing many more stories from his adventures and wealth of knowledge.

I hope this book was able to help you understand and admire the true story of the Rise and the Fall of the Roman Kingdom.

Finally, if you enjoyed it, then I'd like to ask you for a favor, would you be kind enough to leave a review for this book on Amazon? It'd be greatly appreciated!

Thank you again and good luck!

24547904R00064

Printed in Great Britain
by Amazon